Let's Breakup

Poems of Love, Life, and Loss

Jennifer Kain

Copyright©2018 Jennifer Kain
All Rights Reserved

Published by Unsolicited Press
Portland, Oregon
www.unsolicitedpress.com

No part of this book may be reproduced or transmitted in any form or by any means without written permission from the publisher or author.

Printed in the United States of America.

Cover Design: Courtney Mayo

Attention schools and businesses: for discounted copies on large orders, please contact the publisher directly.

ISBN: 978-1-947021-58-7

Table of Contents

DEAR BEST FRIEND	9
DEAR HISTORY	12
DEAR NANA ELIZABETH	16
DEAR GRANDMA DOROTHY	18
SUNFLOWER	19
SEQUOIA TREE	20
DEAR BLUE IPHONE	21
AWAKE	23
GREY PERIOD	24
DEAR WALKING PNEUMONIA	26
DEAR HOUSE ON SEQUOIA DRIVE	29
DEAR TEARS STUCK INSIDE MY EYEBALLS	32
DEAR A RANDOM THURSDAY	34
MOUNTAINTOP	35
CARBOHYDRATES	37
AN ODE TO 2015	39
DEAR GOD	41

Special Thanks

To those I lost. I will never forget you. To everyone else. Hold the people you love close. Our days are numbered.

Let's Breakup

Poems of Love, Life, and Loss

DEAR BEST FRIEND

Remember when we would go to Miles Square Park
and you would teach me how to fly your model airplanes?
How all of the four Bob's would just marvel
at how well you crashed your planes.
How that they all thought if you gave me the chance
I could build a better, lighter plane than you.
I loved when you gave me the transmitter and I saw
this tiny marvel in the sky.

How with a few clicks I would gently guide the plane
to a nearby hill or trees.
"Steady now..." you would say. "Don't go flying over
to the military base. You won't be able to get it back there."
I always wanted to fly it over the military base
to see what would happen.

As time passes I found friends but
they never compared to you.
I would ask you about the glory days
of being in the Navy during World War 2.
And you would tell me that you wouldn't
have survived if it weren't for your appendix bursting.

They took you to an island hospital and made you well.
You never told me how that made you feel; knowing
all of your buddies died while you lived.
You never focused on the horrors of war.
So I didn't either.

Best friend, I met a boy. And he calls me his best friend.
For the longest time, I just told him I was his, too,
because I believed it.
But for some reason there was this fuse always going off
in my stomach when I said it to him.
It's as if I forgot who my best friend was.

I'm tired of breaking up with friends.
You, in particular, I'm angry about.
I had no say in the matter to end our relationship.
Isn't that how it goes?
I hesitate now to call people best friends so quickly.
I never factor in the leaving part.

I think there's a part of me that had to let you go.
I'm slowly discovering the side effects of being your friend.
You were loyal to the very end.
Even in the hospital you squeezed my hand and I knew

that it was good-bye.
I couldn't say good-bye to you.
I will never forget you, Best Friend.

DEAR HISTORY

2015 was a bitch. I'm writing to tell you,
It's inconsequential to others.
But for me
Was the year I knew how the pit of my soul
Crawled up from the cave that was my stomach
And vomited up the tear duct stained truth.

Now I know death is real.
I tried to deny it.
But it happened.

This is the honest truth.
You took something that was universal
And made it personal
And I'm offended.

I have heard many say.
When X was gone the light went out.
My soul lurched for comfort.
History you gave me many days of
Crying, and holding myself under tight covers in my bed.
But you did not give me the warm and fuzzies.

History you taught me,
Everyone will have his or her moment to be remembered.
Even if it's just for an hour.

First you took the matriarch named Nana Elizabeth,
She was a fiery red headed mother of four, strong willed, stubborn, and clever.
My Nana taught me to speak my mind and she liked me for that.
I wasn't the favorite grandchild.
History take note you let another rebel fall asleep, literally in her bed,
Her last breath was on January 9, 2015.
She died at the age of 78.

Then there was the nurse,
Who raised three passionate daughters and at times had more of an animal shelter than a
home.
Her girls housed bunnies, kitties, a few dogs and I'm sure some cold breathing reptile at some point.
History please note she never thought of herself as creative,

But I think in order to raise a scientist, an island dreamer and a fashion culturist you need to have a brave heart and an open ear.

My Grandma Dorothy loved deeply and married her best friend Bob.

She left the Earth February 20, 2015.

She died at the age of 86.

Next was a beautiful, loving, courageous, incredible friend to me and my family,

She fought ALS down to her last days. Both in her body but and in politics,

She made ALS real and deadly to many who didn't understand,

Why ALS sucks,

How her mind could be nimble yet she needed help eating soup

She died April 2, 2015. Jodi was only 45.

Leaving behind her two daughters, a teenage son, and devoted husband.

Lastly in this trail of death was my best friend Grandpa Bob.

History you record that Bob and Dorothy truly loved each other down to the last days. They taught me what true compassion and love of marriage could be,

He passed away June 26th 2015 at the age of 89.

History can you tell me why I'm a paralyzed and unable to move forward or back?

My insides reek and I'm porous,

Any moment now a dam might burst,

And that river might flow out

In the street and a monumental wave might come crashing out

And flood my apartment complex.

You did what you had to do History, but that doesn't mean I approve,

These moments in history shouldn't be here.

History I'm breaking up with you because these things can't be the truth.

You seem to be lying to me even though these deaths are printed in places and on headstones.

Sincerely Yours

DEAR NANA ELIZABETH

Since you've been gone Pappa has taken your chair.
You must have good tastes because he only sits there.
I feel weird sitting in your chair.
Don't you remember which one I am talking about?
The mauve, soft fabric and pillowlike cushion that only a recliner can bring.
There's a part of me that thinks you'll be sitting
in it any day now.

Sweet, wet kisses on wrinkly noses and smoothly,
lined cheeks
At family gatherings.
Which will never be the same.
Your presence always filled a room.
Without it every family function seems
Deflated.

Children cope.
Heavy, mouth breathing, silence at
My cousins bridal shower.
Your presence was felt.
Why weren't you here to see it?

You should've been.
All I feel is the emptiness you left me.

She mattered to you in ways
I will never
Comprehend.

DEAR GRANDMA DOROTHY

I'm sorry I haven't written.

I've been in such a cloud of fog since Grandpa died

It's been such a long time since I experienced you in a fluid non-Alzheimer's state of mind.

There are so many things I wanted to thank you for.

I was such a selfish kid.

Didn't I know one day you would gone?

If only this were the magical world of Harry Potter and when I look at photos of us they would talk.

I still hear your sweet, comforting, mouse like voice in my head.

How it could soothe a hen of chicks to silence and sleep.

It's my time to go.

You are gone.

You broke up with me.

To be honest, I blame Alzheimer's for the breakup.

A dirty disease, fingerling your brain until we were no more.

SUNFLOWER

Sunflower you flow so gently,
In a meadow you fly so perfectly,
Can I rest in your arms once more?
Will there be a next time?
Will there be petals?
I want to stay here forever.
Slowly they will die,
Slowly they will sing,
A song to the one they lost.
The angel went to Heaven today,
She smiles down on you,
Sunflowers in her hair.
I always will smile when I see Sunflowers,
Her grass will always seem cheery to me.
Flowers grow and die,
With each passing moment
I won't forget you Sunflower
You are always blooming
Forever.

SEQUOIA TREE

Why are you so old?
Your rings say 500 years,
You must have been one of the lucky ones,
To avoid the burning and the fires,
When I visit,
We will make tea for two,
I will wait for my friend to show up.
You Sequoia Tree are not invited to tea,
Especially since we are to read about the sea foams,
You don't know how to read Sequoia Tree.
When you eventually die will you live again?
Will you be remembered or forgotten?
I'm told you don't have a memory,
But what about your rings?
If I take a picture of your bark will you be remembered?
There's something mystical,
Your bark is broken and rigid,
If my skin could show how it really feels it would look old
and withered and majestic like
You.
But I know you have millions of stories to tell,
If only your trunk could talk.
Dear Sequoia Tree,
I will not forget thee,
For as long as I live.

DEAR BLUE IPHONE

It's sunny today and warm,
So I wore my shorts and I tried to put you
On silent.
But please. Call me. Message Me.
Get me out of here.

There. You saved me. Thank you.
Thank you for giving me a reason to distract.
Distract away from the pain of knowing.
My grandfather sits hooked up to monitors.
In the ICU.

Whether I wanted to or not.
You told me key deadlines.
I should ignore you.
Delete you.
Throw you in the ocean.
But I won't.
The addiction is intoxicating and I
Can't control it.

In the ICU getting a name tag feels like a badge of honor.
Let's shout from the roof!
But I won't.
People might think I'm crazy if I start screaming.

Whenever I left the start pad I would just switch
        you off into silent.
It's easier to deal with the notion my grandfather
        is slowly dying in
Front of me while you are on silent.
Because of this we are temporarily breaking up.
I need some space and you will only bother me
        from my disillusionment.

AWAKE

As I lay awake,
I can't get thoughts out of my head,
Constant over and over.
Why must he be gone?
Why must I deal with another?
I need peace.
I need rest.
Take my soul oh Lord.
Why is this hard?
The pain cuts deep,
Through my heart and out,
Do they see me?
Do they see I'm crying?
My eyes are wet,
The blanket is wet.
I'm wet.
With sorrow.
I have to move through this moment.
Vacuum cleaners are a comfort,
I blame you for the pictures,
That's all I think about now,
Wheel chair Grandpa,
His many carpet cleaners,
Why am I still awake?

GREY PERIOD

You are my limbo,
It's a space between the lives we live,
I find you in the dark corners of my office.
You are the dust,
The haze that won't leave,
The yearning for something more,
But can't.
Grey I've become acquainted with you,
To say it's comfortable
Is a lie,
I would rather tie you up,
Throw you in the Pacific Ocean,
Watch you fall deep into the Mariana's Trench.
But I can't touch you.
Like most events,
I can't hold events hostage,
They are nebulous feelings.
I wish I visited more,
I wish I called,
I wish I did more with you.
Regrets, guilt and sadness,
The grey period thrives on

Emotions that get stuck in the cracks.
I'm breaking up,
Breaking up with you,
Grey period we are breaking up
Get out,
I'm done.

DEAR WALKING PNEUMONIA

Some would say that your arrival is tragic,
But I say bring it on.
You are helping me avoid,
It's giving me a goal to focus on.
The breath in my lungs,
Slowly filling up the fluid,
I can't do this.
This breathing treatment,
This PTSD. I'm not my Grandpa. COPD is not Pneumonia,
Two Weeks. Two Weeks and this.
It's never ending.
This silent sickness. It finally creeped out.

It makes sense that you're floating around in my body.
I'm just unable to deal.
The job. The thesis. The four deaths.
In a six month period.
My body is your wasteland,
I let you invade no problem.
The longer I have you living inside of me,
The stronger I get mentally

The vulnerable seepage of my heart,

Wake up.
You're my Elder and I have to hold onto your hand,
While crossing that street.
Because quite literally it's hard to walk a few feet,
Without feeling dizzy.

In the bathroom I'm kneeling on the floor,
Feeling the cold, cool porcelain against my cheek,
My chest is hollow,
All I can see is my rib cage bones.

No other organs exist except you,
Lungs.
You lungs are just sad, shriveled and crying,
Black tears.

I just want to swim,
In the black sea of my sack of lungs.
All comfy and squished in.
An amoeba of feeling.

The 100 degrees outside,
The lack of AC inside,
Drives the Los Angeles Angel in Me a bit
Mad.

Water droplets of sweat,
Pool around my eyes, knee caps and arms.
You have forced me to stay inside,
Not walking or doing anything fun.

You're a horrible thing, you know that?
Why is your soul purpose to reproduce and multiply?

By day 15 I'm so ready to throw in the towel with you.
I miss eating food, drinking coffee and walking without feeling dizzy.
To put it plainly, you suck and it's time for us to break up.
I don't want you to come back and it wasn't worth the relationship.
I survived, but you lasted quite some time inside of me. I hope it was worth it.
Good-bye forever.

DEAR HOUSE ON SEQUOIA DRIVE

Today was the last day I walked through your frame to grace   your wooden presence.
To be honest I'm not going to miss you
You collected spider webs, dust, dirt and whatever else.

I honor you today.
Even as I write to you.
The notebook I'm writing in has a door on the front.
It looks like a secret garden door with whimsical vines and an   old stonewall.
The door I imagine is wooden with a cast iron latch.
It's everything a door should be.
All doors are special because inside is where all the stories get told.

Are you a time machine?
Grandpa and Grandma will be back home soon.
Even though the hospital bed was warm.
I know that it will be empty once more.

This is a rational thought.
Don't fight me on this.
Walls see the stories others can't.
The end of being able to drive to you,
Is the death of a part of my soul.

Grief does that.
Not that you've experienced it Sequoia House.
You're the last piece of my childhood.
The last safe haven.
I'm not ready to leave you.

I'm stalling to end this because even writing this means the loss of you.
It's not like your walls were made of perfection or lollipops, but it's about the memories.
The first time I learned to sew was in Lynn's room on the singer sewing machine from the 50s.
The first time grandpa played the organ and I knew it sounded way better than a piano.
Or the first time Gran and I sat in the kitchen and we made our first batch of cookies.
You save all of this. And for that I'm grateful.
You saw fights, tantrums and family meals and you never judged us.

I have to let you go because I must continue my day.

Leaving you isn't the same as forgetting you.

But sadly, it dawns on me.....

Grandpa Bob and Grandma Dorothy are not ever coming home.

They have died and I must accept this.

I guess that's why it's come to my attention that we must break up.

It's not you, it's me. I need to work on myself in becoming a better me.

You like that one?

My dear house that I might never walk into again,

I love you,

I respect you and I acknowledge how you feel,

but we must break up.

DEAR TEARS STUCK INSIDE MY EYEBALLS

Why can't you just come flowing outside and
onto my cheeks?
My cheeks are in need of you, tears.
Are you afraid if you cry in public people will look at you?
Yes, they will look at you, but screw them.
You don't need them.
If you feel like shit because everywhere you look all you
      think about is your Grandfather,
Then so be it.
You can't control when you're going to think about him,
So intensely and all you want to do is hug him,
For one last time and hear his voice.

Let those tears start flowing.
When you don't go and see someone to talk to about your
      thoughts and feelings
these days will just come and you're going to have to
      deal with it.
The more you push back these thoughts and
      feelings the worse
it's going to be the day you burst.

The day you burst you will be in the middle of a grocery store   looking at cantaloupes

These tears will just be weird and nobody will be around,

To give you a hug and tell you it's okay if you keep it up.

Tears, I'm serious. You need to get over yourselves.

It's your mental health that's going to hell if you just keep doing this.

Holding in the pain works occasionally until it migrates into   something else.

Releasing emotion and letting water flow onto the cheeks are just part of life.

The cheeks need the flow of water to feel used.

It's time you break out and not up.

Let your water flow.

Sincerely a very stubborn person.

DEAR A RANDOM THURSDAY

I don't need your hipsters,
Your cool cars or hilly locations,
I don't need your rain,
Your vegan chili,
Or your sympathy.
I'm fine and I don't need a support group.
But The Dinner Party found me.
It broke the barriers,
I cried. We ate.
For the first time I didn't feel.
Crazy. But
Normal.
Thursday we must break up because you
Are only but twenty-four hours,
But I won't forget you.
The Dinner Partier

MOUNTAINTOP

I seek your snowcapped peace,
It's quiet up there,
Just with the animals,
I find you,
I need quiet.
Quiet seems to never be around,
From screaming babies,
To loud traffic.
Where do I find quiet Mountaintop?
Snow, ice, sheep,
Not a peep.
Silence.
Airports, jet's landing,
Fuel,
Propellers.
Why didn't Grandpa ever teach me how to build,
Model airplanes.
I wish.
I wish I asked,
I wish I took more time,
I wish I didn't let my last year get away from me,
Why didn't I ask,

He would have helped,
Planes were his past.
Not mine.
I wanted to be like him,
To build little planes,
To be better than him,
Protégé is overrated,
I would've loved to be overrated.
He would've been proud of me.
That's all gone now.
Where's his propellers?
Where's his spirit.
Have you seen any planes lately?

CARBOHYDRATES

Why must you be so fattening and delicious?
The golden-brown crust,
The butter and sprinkles.
Footsteps and wheels,
Geocaching and red SUV's,
Busy parking lots and smiles.
Old pasty skin,
Hand holding,
Locked eyes.
Lovers and carbs,
A match made in Heaven,
Booths over tables.
Sunshine and lemon-flavored pancakes,
Anaheim makes for the best,
Adventures.
Saturday mornings,
Longing for food,
Long lines and lots of stories.

Missing you,
Missing your voice and your spirit.
I look at pictures on the menu first,

Because of you.
Pictures on menus are important,
It's how Grandpa always made
Decisions.
Calories didn't matter,
Carbohydrates are King.

AN ODE TO 2015

It's been a year of old and new,
Sadness and triumph.
Each time it's new and I'm older.
From the past that brings me an ancient art of memories,
To the future my mind is blank and filled up with hope,
Fearlessly I go into the great blue yonder,
For who is to come is the greatest mystery,

From funerals to parties and wineries,
To ends of lives and new beginnings,
Friendship is a circle it always comes back,
Sometimes new and unexpected.
To diploma's and thesis publications,
To acceptances and realizations,
To reality and dreams and knowing the difference between the two.
To finding happiness through sorrow,
To being okay with tears,
Acceptance is key
Crying in the Laundromat,
Accept it.
People are unaware.

To rain, illness and long distances,
To weddings, smiles and rings,
Finding solace in the moment
Is worth a thousand seconds in heaven.
To heartbeats, and weird fruit,
To hospitals and cell phones,
Seeking comfort where there is none,
Cuts the heart in half.

To 2015 a year for the making,
To world series games and almost wishes,
To hiding away from the world,
To fireworks and love.
To Living in the Moment,
Loving the Past,
And cherishing the laughter
Today.

Good night dear one. You won't be forgotten.

DEAR GOD

Dear King of Kings,
Lord of Lords!
Jesus? Sir?
Big Man in the stars?
Are you there?
Typical.
First step.
People leave when they aren't ready.
 It's not my job to save them.
John 11:35 "Jesus wept"
Should I pause and take a moment and forgive?
You forgave my broken soul.
With great love.
In order to be free I must let it go.
Let go the sorrow, pain, and guilt,
Start embracing freedom of the soul.
Praise is to you oh Lord.
Amen.

About the Author

A bit of a wanderer. Jennifer Kain runs an online magazine called <u>The Articles of Antiquity</u> founded in 2013 which focuses on interviews, reviews, and commentaries about entertainment and media culture. When she's not furiously writing for her magazine, she's always in search for the best taco and finding peace in the midst of the storm. Which usually is next to a tall shady tree.

About the Press

UNSOLICITED PRESS is a small press in Portland, Oregon. It is driven by a sparkling team of volunteers who seek to produce outstanding poetry, fiction, and creative nonfiction. Learn more at www.unsolicitedpress.com.

www.ingramcontent.com/pod-product-compliance
Lightning Source LLC
Chambersburg PA
CBHW052107110526
44591CB00013B/2382